KNOWLEDGE ENCYCLOPEDIA

MEDICAL INVENTIONS

INVENTIONS & DISCOVERIES

(An imprint of Prakash Books Pvt. Ltd.)

Wonder House Books
Corporate & Editorial Office
113-A, 1st Floor, Ansari Road,
Daryaganj, New Delhi-110002
Tel +91 11 2324 7062-65

Printed in 2020 in India

ISBN : 9789390391196

Table of Contents

MEDICAL MARVELS

In ancient times, human beings believed that disease was not natural, but rather, a supernatural phenomenon. Diseases were thought to be the result of an enemy's curse or a sign of God's displeasure. They could even signify that you were possessed by a demon. Thus, the earliest doctors were also sorcerers!

In the 5th century BCE, doctors began to set aside superstition and looked for physical causes of illnesses. Great leaps in medicine were made in the Middle East during the Middle Ages. Finally, in the 19th century, microorganisms like bacteria and viruses were identified as agents of disease. Since then, life-saving inventions in the medical field mark some of the most extraordinary achievements of humankind.

◀ *Specialised teams of doctors and scientists have been the reason behind many medical miracles*

A Peek Inside the Body

When doctors first began to look for natural causes of illnesses, they did not have the proper tools to help them. Devices like the thermometer and stethoscope had not been invented. So, doctors had to use their eyes and ears to observe patients and diagnose diseases.

Modern Medical Equipment

These days, medical experts have hi-tech imaging equipment that shows what is happening inside a patient's body. Such technologies include X-ray, ultrasound and MRI. Other machines like the **EEG** and **ECG** chart our brain waves and heartbeats, so doctors can tell if they are functioning normally.

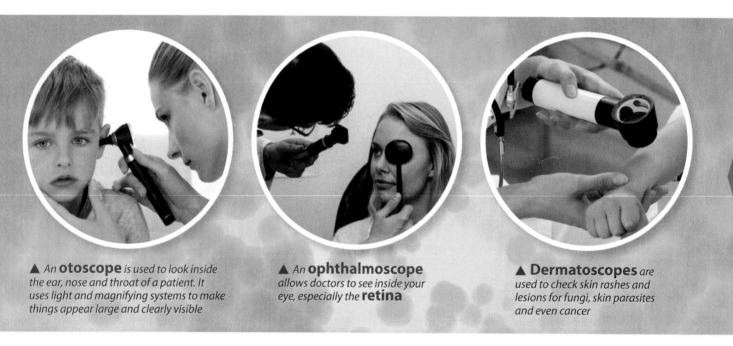

▲ An **otoscope** is used to look inside the ear, nose and throat of a patient. It uses light and magnifying systems to make things appear large and clearly visible

▲ An **ophthalmoscope** allows doctors to see inside your eye, especially the **retina**

▲ **Dermatoscopes** are used to check skin rashes and lesions for fungi, skin parasites and even cancer

Checking Your Temperature

When you feel ill, the first thing to do is to check if you have a fever. The tool with which you measure your body temperature is called a thermometer. The Italian mathematician Galileo Galilei invented the earliest known thermometer in 1592. The first accurate mercury thermometer was created in 1714 by German physicist Daniel Gabriel Fahrenheit. The Fahrenheit scale of temperature measurement, in which ice melts at 32° F and the temperature of a healthy human body is 96° F, was named after him. In 1942, Swedish astronomer Anders Celsius gave us the other popular scale, the centigrade or Celsius.

▲ A patient using a modern digital thermometer

◀ When heated, the air inside the glass tube of Galileo's thermometer expands, changing the level of the liquid. The glass bulbs carry temperature markers corresponding to the liquid

🔅 Isn't It Amazing!

Celsius originally used 0° C as the boiling point of water and 100° C as the melting point of snow. It was later turned around and became more popular with 0° C as the melting point of ice and 100° C the boiling point of water.

▲ A mercury thermometer showing measurements in both Celsius and Fahrenheit

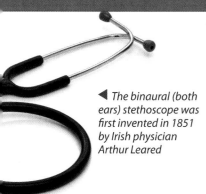

◀ *The binaural (both ears) stethoscope was first invented in 1851 by Irish physician Arthur Leared*

Listening to the Body

The first stethoscope was invented in 1816 by French physician Rene Theophile Hyacinthe Laennec. The stethoscope allows doctors to clearly listen to sounds within a patient's body. Most often, doctors listen to the sounds made by the heart and lungs using the stethoscope.

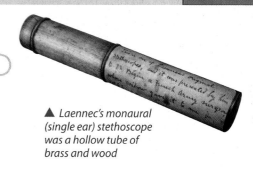

▲ *Laennec's monaural (single ear) stethoscope was a hollow tube of brass and wood*

Digital Thermometers

Nowadays, mercury thermometers are being replaced by digital models. Digital thermometers work by using a thermistor—a material whose resistance to electricity changes with changing temperatures. This resistance is measured by a computer chip inside the thermometer. The measurement is converted into a temperature reading, which is then shown to us on a display screen.

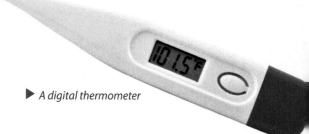

▶ *A digital thermometer*

Measuring Blood Pressure

A healthy heart is necessary for pumping blood throughout the body. When blood is pushed into blood vessels, it naturally presses against the walls of the vessels. This pressure is measured using a machine called a **sphygmomanometer**. Blood pressure can be affected by a huge number of illnesses. It is, therefore, one of the first things that doctors check to understand the state of your health. The first useful sphygmomanometer was invented by Austrian physician Karl Samuel Ritter von Basch in 1881.

An inflatable pad on the sphygmomanometer is wrapped around your upper arm and air is pumped through it, until it squeezes your arm. The doctor then measures your blood pressure using a stethoscope and the measuring counter attached to the sphygmomanometer.

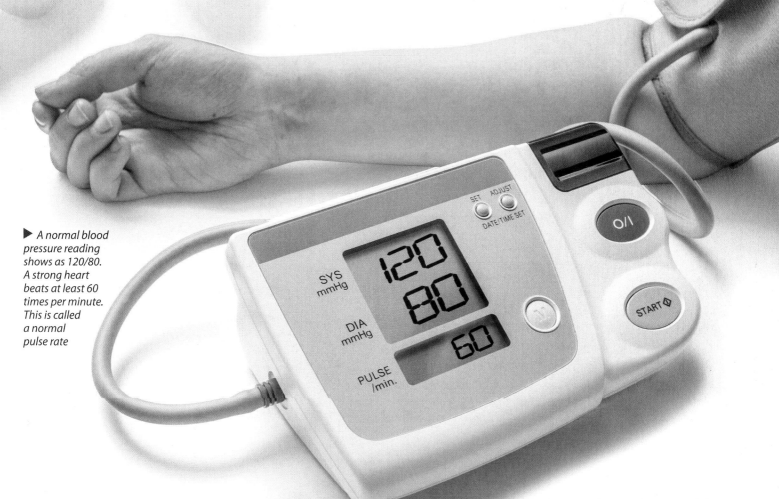

▶ *A normal blood pressure reading shows as 120/80. A strong heart beats at least 60 times per minute. This is called a normal pulse rate*

Photography for Physicians

Colours are made of electromagnetic rays called light. Apart from light, there are numerous other electromagnetic waves that are invisible to our eyes. Light cannot get into and out of our body, but certain sounds and electromagnetic waves can. Using these, inventors have built incredible machines to 'photograph' what is inside the body. Such imaging devices are used by doctors to diagnose your illness without cutting you open.

▲ *This image shows a series of MRI scans of the brain from different angles*

🔍 The Invisible X Factor

In 1895, German physicist Wilhelm Röntgen first discovered the presence of invisible **electromagnetic rays**. He called these mysterious waves X-rays. Unlike light, X-rays can pass through our bodies, but only through some parts. Bones and dense tissue are too thick for X-rays to penetrate.

If you put a piece of photographic film in the background, the X-rays that pass through the patient will hit the film and turn it black. The parts of the body that stop X-rays from going through will be outlined in white. Thus, X-ray photographs are used to look for damaged hard tissues, such as bone fractures.

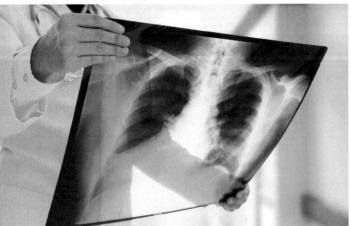

◀ *An X-ray film of the chest cavity; bones of the rib cage, spine and shoulders appear in white*

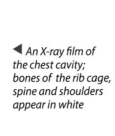

▶ *The first Nobel Prize for Physics was given to Röntgen in 1901, for his extraordinary discovery of invisible rays all around us. It ushered in a new era for physics and revolutionised medicine*

🔍 CT Scan

A Computed Tomography (CT) scan is a special type of X-ray machine. It was developed in the 1970s by Godfrey Newbold Hounsfield and Allan MacLeod Cormack, who shared a Nobel Prize for it in 1979. CT scans are popular in medicine for their detailed, high-resolution images. More importantly, they are able to photograph cross-sections of organs, so doctors can see what your organs look like from the inside.

⭐ Incredible Individuals

During WWII, a brilliant scientist named Marie Curie equipped vans with X-ray machines, so doctors could look for bullets inside wounded soldiers. The vans were fondly called 'petites Curies' (little Curies).

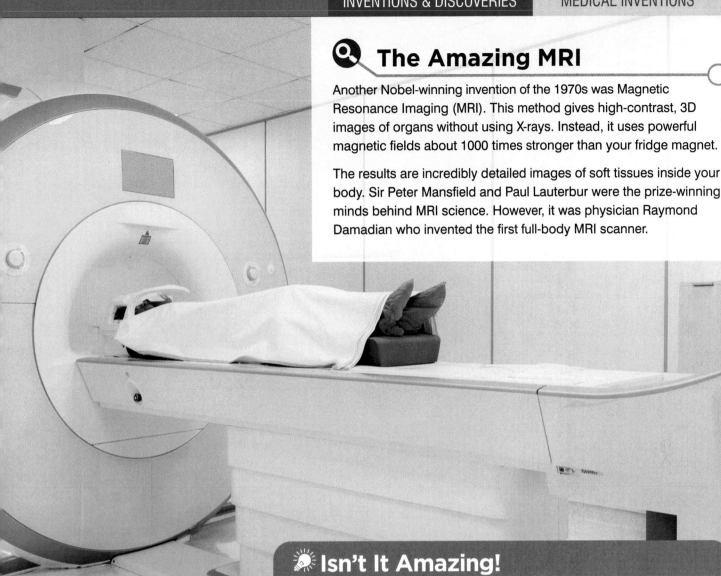

The Amazing MRI

Another Nobel-winning invention of the 1970s was Magnetic Resonance Imaging (MRI). This method gives high-contrast, 3D images of organs without using X-rays. Instead, it uses powerful magnetic fields about 1000 times stronger than your fridge magnet.

The results are incredibly detailed images of soft tissues inside your body. Sir Peter Mansfield and Paul Lauterbur were the prize-winning minds behind MRI science. However, it was physician Raymond Damadian who invented the first full-body MRI scanner.

▲ During an MRI scan, the patient lies very still inside a large cylindrical machine that creates steady and strong magnetic fields

Isn't It Amazing!

It might seem strange now, but the idea for ultrasonography actually came from ships. Specifically, the idea for the ultrasound machine came from an instrument that was used to detect flaws in ships! In the 1950s, Scottish physician Ian Donald and engineer Tom Brown invented the ultrasound prototype for use in **obstetrics**.

Ultrasonography

Very high-pitched sounds are called ultrasounds. Some animals, like bats and whales, use ultrasound to visualise their surroundings! Likewise, doctors use ultrasound machines to look inside patients.

The machine sends ultrasound waves into the body. The sound that bounces back after hitting body tissue is called the echo. Different intensities of echoes are used by the machine to understand the relative position of tissues. This information is used to create an image of the tissues inside the body.

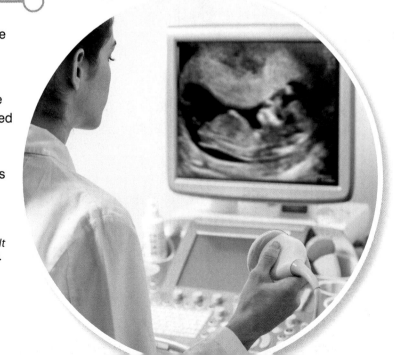

▶ Unlike X-rays, there are no health risks associated with ultrasound. It is therefore used to check the health of a baby inside a mother's womb. CT scans and MRIs are also prohibited for pregnant women

Testing Patients

Doctors often take blood and urine samples to diagnose deficiencies and infections in body tissue or fluids. Our blood may look red, but it is largely made up of a pale yellowish liquid called plasma. The red colour comes from red blood cells, which carry oxygen to different parts of our body. There are also white blood cells, which fight diseases, and platelets which form blood clots when we get hurt.

Why Take a Blood Test?

In a healthy body, all the elements of the blood, such as the white blood cells and red blood cells, are in balance. When the count of any one of them changes, it is a sure sign of illness. In particular, when your body is fighting a bacterial or viral infection, the number of white blood cells will show marked changes.

A Transport System

Blood vessels are like highways of the human body, transporting chemicals from one place to another. They carry nutrients from your gut (where food is digested) to the rest of the body. Therefore, blood tests for glucose, vitamins and minerals can show if your body is correctly absorbing nutrients from the food you eat. Also present are hormones, which are special substances that affect your growth, emotions, energy and other aspects of a normal life. Tests for these chemicals diagnose a wide range of serious illnesses, including the increasingly common condition, diabetes (related to the hormone insulin).

▶ *The most common ailment related to red blood cells is anaemia, where a person suffers from a deficiency of red blood cells or haemoglobin in the body. They may thus appear unhealthily pale or yellow*

⊙ Incredible Individuals

King Philippe-Auguste (1165–1223) of France had a doctor called Gilles de Corbeil, who described 20 different types of urine. A good teacher, de Corbeil turned his observations into *Poem on the Judgment of Urines*, so his students of medicine could memorise it all easily. The poem was popular for centuries.

Understanding Urine

On either side of our body, just where the ribcage ends, is a fist-sized organ called the kidney. The kidneys filter waste from the blood and send it out in the form of urine. At the same time, they ensure that things that are of use to the body, such as salts, water, and protein, go back into the blood. Most urine tests will, therefore, look for abnormal amounts of sugar, protein, **bilirubin**, blood cells and foreign bodies like bacteria. This reflects the overall health of the blood, kidneys and urinary tract.

▲ *Urine culture refers to growing microorganisms present in urine in a petri dish, and it is used to check for abnormal bacteria. Gram-negative bacilli, seen here, are a group of bacteria responsible for many diseases including diarrhoea, cholera, plague and typhoid*

In Real Life

There are many different kinds of blood tests. A Complete Blood Count (CBC) checks that you have the right proportion of cells in your blood. It can reflect disorders like anaemia, blood cancer and problems with your immunity or clotting mechanism. Other basic tests include Blood Enzyme Tests and Blood Chemistry Tests.

Testing Waste Matter

From very early on, human beings have been obsessed with checking, testing and making notes on excrement. From such records, we know that the famously mad King George III of England may have suffered from **porphyria**, an illness that produces blue urine. However, the king was being treated with gentian at the time. So, it is also conjectured that the deep blue flowers of the plant might have given an unnatural colour to his urine.

Undeniably, waste matter from our bodies can reveal a great deal to our doctors. Thus, urine tests are a standard part of health check-ups in modern times.

The Need for Biopsy

To examine ailing organs, doctors may remove some sample tissue and look at it under a microscope. This is called a **biopsy**. The first biopsy to diagnose an illness was done in Russia in 1875 by M. M. Rudnev.

The simplest form of a biopsy today uses a needle to extract sample tissue. This is done for tissue that is just under your skin. More complex processes are involved in removing samples from deep within your body.

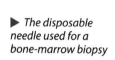

▶ The disposable needle used for a bone-marrow biopsy

 ## The Syringe

The earliest known syringe-like device was used in Rome in the first century. During the ninth century CE, an Egyptian surgeon invented a suction syringe made of a hollow glass tube. It was only in 1946 that an all-glass syringe was invented. The hollow needle of the syringe was invented by Irish physician Francis Rynd. It was further refined by Charles Pravaz and Alexander Wood in 1853. In 1949, Australian Charles Rothauser created the first disposable plastic syringe.

In Real Life

Hypodermic needles are an important invention as they are extremely hygienic and reduce chances of infection. The needle is so smooth that germs in the air do not get trapped on its surface. Also, the sharp needle creates a small puncture in your skin, which heals quickly, so germs cannot get in.

▼ In a hospital, water, glucose, antibiotics and other medicines are often sent directly to your blood by inserting a syringe in your arm and connecting it to the bottle of fluids with a tube. This is called Intravenous (IV) therapy

▼ Modern microscopes can send images of the tissue biopsy to computer screens for better visibility

⊛ Incredible Individuals

Alexander Wood used the hypodermic syringe to experiment with morphine, a drug that can relieve pain but, if taken in large doses, can also cause death. There is a rumour about him and his wife Rebecca Massey. It is said that the couple experimented by injecting morphine into their own bodies. They supposedly became addicted to the drug and the unfortunate Rebecca Massey became the first woman to die of a drug overdose from an injection. While this might just be a tale, it is true that many people had become addicted to morphine. In fact, during the American Civil War, addiction to morphine came to be known as the 'soldier's disease'.

🔍 Microscope

It is an invention that makes tiny objects appear large, so that they can be examined properly. The device consists of two or more lenses that can be adjusted for clarity. The magnifying power of a microscope refers to how much it can visually enlarge an object. For instance, the notation '10x' means that the microscope can magnify an object to 10 times its original size.

▲ *The handheld magnifying glass can show images that are 20 times (20x) larger than the original. A single-lens microscope can magnify up to 300x. Compound microscopes can magnify up to 2,000x*

🔍 The Electron Microscope

Most microscopes use light to show enlarged images. The electron microscope (EM) uses a beam of electrons to do the same. Since electrons cannot travel far in the air, an EM requires airless space (vacuum) to function properly. This is well worth the trouble, as the magnifying power of EMs is extremely high (about 10,00,000x).

▶ *Images from a microscope can be photographed using a method called* **photomicrography**

🔍 Inventing the EM

In 1931, Max Knoll and Ernst Ruska—both electrical engineers—built the first EM. It was a two-lens microscope that directly photographed the source of the electrons. Two years later, another EM first took an enlarged picture of an object. Finally, in 1935, Knoll was able to scan a solid surface using an EM.

▶ *A researcher using a modern electronic microscope*

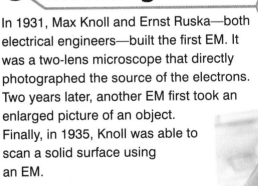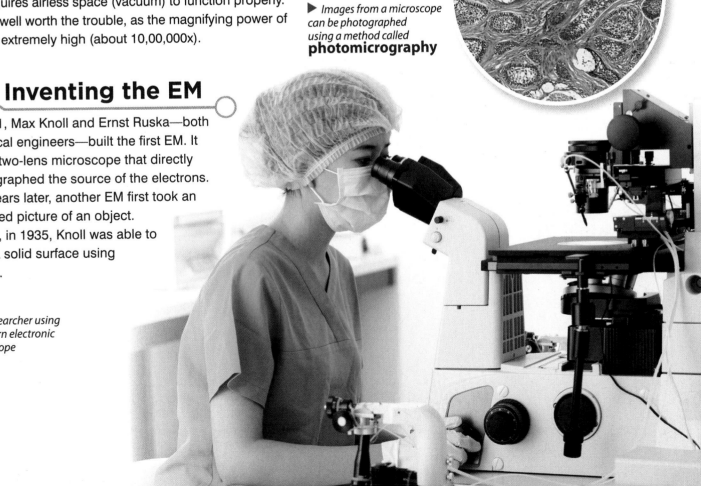

A History of Hygiene

In Greek mythology, Hygeia is the Goddess of health and the daughter of Aesculapius, the God of medicine. Although ancient civilisations did not know about germs, they understood that cleanliness and hygiene are linked to health.

🔍 A Timeline on Sanitation

Human beings of the very first civilisations (such as Indus Valley and Mesopotamia) were already building sewage systems, in order to dispose of waste in a safe manner. Of course, once the **germ theory** of the 19th century took root, doctors and governments worked hard to put strong hygiene practices in place.

2nd millennium BCE

Toilets are used in India, China and other parts of the world. These are different from modern toilets.

1550–1200 BCE

Egyptians mix oils and salts to form a type of soap used to cure skin diseases.

3rd millennium BCE

Sanitation networks are made using brick and clay pipes to take sewage outside the cities. Medicinal sticks from certain trees are used to clean teeth. In ancient Rome, the rich pay to obtain clean drinking water.

2800 BCE

Soap-like products are seen in ancient Babylon.

▶ *The Indus Valley residents used bathing centres, wells and water reserves to ensure hygiene*

👤 In Real Life

King James VI of Scotland (1473–1513) was an energetic man who unified his country and made it wealthy. He was not particularly hygienic though. He did not take bath, believing it was bad for health. In fact, he wore the same clothes for months and even slept in them sometimes.

▲ *King James VI*

💡 Isn't It Amazing!

Romans thought that urine was an excellent stain remover and even used it as a teeth whitener at one point. Even during medieval times, people used a mixture of ashes and urine (called chamber lye) to clean clothes.

1498 BCE

The first bristle toothbrush is used in China. It is made of a bamboo handle with hair from a hog's neck.

▲ *This toothbrush made for Napoleon Bonaparte dates back to 1795*

600 BCE

Greeks begin using public baths and chamber pots (non-flushing toilets).

A doctor called Ignaz Semmelweis discovered that his students were handling corpses and births at the same time. He insisted that the students wash their hands after tending to dead bodies. Within three months, deaths of newborn babies and their mothers had dropped by 20 times!

▲ *A statue of Semmelweis in front of a hospital in Hungary*

400 CE

In Britain, people begin using vinegar, mint and water as mouthwash. A concoction of bay leaves in orange flower water is also used for this purpose.

300 BCE

Rich Romans begin using wool and rosewater to wipe their bottoms. A century later, common people use sponges soaked in saltwater.

851 CE

Toilet paper is invented in China.

1819

A system that allows a toilet to flush properly is built. Unfortunately, it cannot be used due to a lack of running water.

1846

Britain faces a scarcity of firewood. As a result, hot baths become very expensive. Families and friends begin sharing bathwater or simply remain dirty.

18th century CE

The first dental chairs and dentures are invented. The latter consist of gold crowns and porcelain teeth. In 1790, a foot engine that rotates a drill for cleaning cavities is invented.

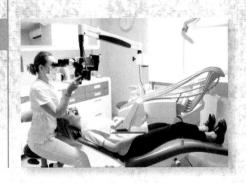

1861

The modern flushing toilet comes into use.

Preventing Infections

Most diseases that spread from person to person are caused by bacteria and viruses. If the infection is not too serious, our bodies are able to create chemicals called antibodies that fight off the disease. But wouldn't it be great if we had antibodies even before the infection? Then the disease would not affect us at all.

🔍 The Miracle of Vaccination

Vaccines are made up of weak or dead bacteria and viruses. They trick our body into thinking that it is being infected. The body then starts producing protective antibodies, even though we are not really ill.

Before vaccines, people used **variolation** (or inoculation) to prevent infections. This was done by applying old scabs or pus from infected boils on to a healthy person. The body responded by producing antibodies.

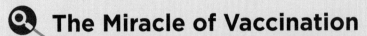

1000–1700 CE

Records from this time describe how people in China and India inoculated against the smallpox virus.

1796

Edward Jenner inoculates eight-year-old James Phipps with cowpox, a mild virus that spreads from cows to people. This breakthrough technique protects Phipps from the deadly smallpox virus. Jenner thus introduces vaccines to the world.

1805

Napoleon Bonaparte's sister Maria Anna Elisa Bonaparte becomes the first ruler to try to make vaccination mandatory. However, her initiative fails due to a lack of feasible methods to make the vaccination process compulsory.

1884

Louis Pasteur creates a vaccine that protects dogs from the fatal rabies virus. The following year, he saves a badly bitten nine-year-old boy named Joseph Meister, with a course of 13 rabies injections.

1885

Pasteur's student Jaime Ferran develops the first anti-cholera vaccine. During a cholera epidemic in Spain, he undertakes the first mass vaccination of some 50,000 people.

▼ An illustration of Dr Edward Jenner injecting young James Phipps with the cowpox virus

▲ Maria Anna Elisa Bonaparte (1777–1820)

▲ Louis Pasteur

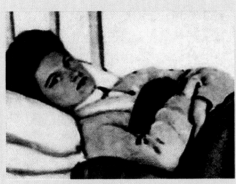

▲ An American maid named Mary Mallon became infamous as 'Typhoid Mary' in the 19th century. She knew she was ill, but continued to work at various households due to ignorance. By the time she was diagnosed, at least 51 people had been infected

⊙ Incredible Individuals

In 1661, China's Emperor Kangxi came to power when his father died of smallpox. Emperor Kangxi himself had survived the disease as a child. Therefore, he had his sons and daughters inoculated against the disease. The successful procedures made him a firm supporter of the practice.

▶ The Qing Dynasty's fourth ruler, Emperor Kangxi

1890s
British bacteriologist Sir Almroth Edward Wright invents an effective vaccine against typhoid. In 1899, the British army tests it on 3,000 soldiers in India during the Second Boer War.

1921
After 13 years of research, French scientists Albert Calmette and Camille Guerin develop the tuberculosis vaccine, calling it BCG (Bacillus Calmette-Guerin).

1936
Max Theiler creates the Yellow Fever vaccine, for which he later receives the Nobel Prize, becoming the only person to win the prize for the invention of a virus vaccine.

1938
Jonas Salk and Thomas Francis invent the first vaccine against influenza. It is used to protect US armed forces during WWII.

1939
American duo Pearl Kendrick and Grace Eldering develop the first effective vaccine for the deadly whooping cough.

1955
Jonas Salk's polio injection is approved. It is replaced in the 60s by an oral vaccine created by Albert Sabin.

1963
Dr John Enders and his team develop a safe measles vaccine.

2005
Measles, mumps, rubella and varicella are now combated using a single MMRV vaccine.

▲ The horse-drawn ambulance used during the last Yellow Fever epidemic in New Orleans, USA

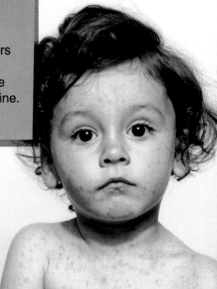

▶ A boy infected with measles

An Infectious Theory

Antibiotics are chemicals produced by living creatures, which can affect the growth of other microorganisms. The chemicals are used to kill disease-causing microorganisms like bacteria. Before their invention, a great many people died from badly infected wounds. Even after bacteria were discovered in the 17th century, many doctors did not believe in their ability to cause infections.

Finally, in the 19th century, people were convinced that infections were caused by invisibly small organisms. The three heroes responsible for this achievement were Louis Pasteur, English surgeon Joseph Lister and German physician Robert Koch.

▼ *Salmonella is a group of rod-shaped bacteria that cause many types of diseases, notably typhoid and food poisoning*

💡 Isn't It Amazing!

Although we think of microbes as harmful creatures, our bodies survive by hosting a wide variety of microbes. For instance, without a healthy population of bacteria in our gut, we wouldn't be able to digest our food properly. Many scientists now believe that being obsessively hygienic destroys good microbes and leads to issues like asthma, skin conditions and allergies.

◀ *The greenish mould (a fungus) penicillium produces the invaluable antibiotic penicillin*

▲ *The Human Immunodeficiency Virus (HIV) is one of the deadliest viral diseases, as it takes away the body's ability to protect itself*

🔍 From Stale to Sterile: Penicillin

Antibiotics gained prominence during the 1940s, thanks to penicillin taken from the fungus penicillium. This powerful antibiotic was popularised by Alexander Fleming, Howard Florey and Ernst Chain. All three shared a Nobel Prize for it in 1945. However, penicillin was not the first antibiotic to be discovered. Nor was Fleming the first person to discover penicillin.

🔍 Alexander Fleming

After he returned from a long holiday, Fleming set about clearing out some petri dishes in his lab. The dishes contained colonies of a deadly bacteria called *staphylococcus*. Somehow, a fungal mould had entered the bacterial culture. Fleming noticed that the mould was producing a 'juice' that was killing the bacteria. He got his assistants to isolate this liquid and studied its properties. It turned out to be the antibiotic penicillin.

🔍 A History of Antibiotics

Though they did not know about bacteria, people in ancient Egypt, China, Greece and Rome knew how to use antibiotics. They used mouldy bread (which releases antibiotic chemicals) to treat infected wounds.

In the 19th century, Rudolf Emmerich and Oscar Low isolated pyocyanase from a green bacterium found in injured people's bandages. When this antibiotic was used in hospitals, different patients displayed different reactions and some even felt no difference.

In 1909, German physician Paul Ehrlich discovered the chemical arsphenamine, a successful cure for adults affected by the syphilis bacteria. Arsphenamine became the predecessor of the modern antibiotic.

▲ *Paul Ehrlich in his lab*

⊙ Incredible Individuals

Most schools teach us that penicillin was discovered in 1928 by Alexander Fleming. But this may not be true. In 1870, Sir John Scott Burdon-Sanderson noted that certain types of mould stopped bacteria from growing. Soon after, Joseph Lister experimented on penicillium and proved its anti-bacterial effect on human tissue. In 1875, John Tyndall also presented his experiments with penicillium. Most importantly, in 1897, Ernest Duchesne saw Arab stable boys applying mould from horse saddles on to their own saddle sores as a cure. He found that this mould was indeed penicillium and used it to successfully cure typhoid fever in guinea pigs.

🔍 The Works of Louis Pasteur

Little was known about microorganisms in the early 19th century. It was French chemist and microbiologist Louis Pasteur (1822–1895) who proved that germs were living beings. He discovered that milk turned sour because of microbes like bacteria. Further, heating milk killed the bacteria and made it safer to drink. This process is called pasteurisation. It is now a standard practice for many foods and drinks. Pasteur's idea also led to the boiling of instruments before surgery, to rid them of infectious bacteria. Most importantly, his work led to the development of vaccines against infectious diseases.

▲ *Portrait of Louis Pasteur in his lab*

Indispensable Medicine

The 20th century saw groundbreaking advances in the invention of medicines. As a result, the average human life is much improved and the human lifespan is steadily increasing. We live longer, healthier lives thanks to the medicinal marvels of the 20th century.

Allergies

When foreign substances enter our body, our immune system responds in a variety of ways to remove them. A strong immune system thus protects us from parasites and microbes. But sometimes, harmless bits of fluff may enter our bodies and cause the system to react. This unnecessary response is called an allergy.

Common things that cause allergies include pollen from flowers, dust, pet hair, insect bites, and even some foods like peanuts and shellfish. The term allergy was coined in 1905 by Austrian physician Clemens von Pirquet.

⊙ Incredible Individuals

Clemens von Pirquet was an Austrian physician. He invented a test for tuberculosis. In this test, a drop of a bacterial protein called tuberculin is scratched on to the surface of the skin. If the area becomes red and raised, it confirms that the person is infected with tuberculosis. In 1909, he showed that more than 90 per cent of the Viennese children he had tested were infected by the disease by the age of 14.

Pirquet also discovered serum sickness, a mild allergic reaction to an injection of serum. This eventually led him to coin and define the term 'allergy'.

▲ People can take tests to find out what they might be allergic to

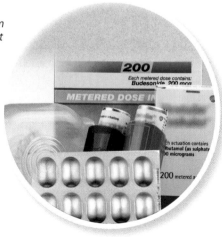

▶ People suffering from allergies must keep anti-allergens handy

🔍 Tackling Allergies

Allergies have existed since ancient times, affecting rich and poor alike. Famously, the Roman emperor Claudius was terribly allergic to his own horse! Allergies can be as mild as a bout of sneezing and deadly enough to cause shock and death.

Unfortunately, we are yet to find a permanent cure for allergies. However, it is easy enough to control them by using medicines called anti-allergens. These range from injections to ointments, tablets and inhalers. Mild anti-allergens like Benadryl (used for hay fever, hives and motion sickness) are easily available at pharmacies.

Pain Relief

Any drug that takes away your pain without putting you instantly to sleep is called an **analgesic**. The best-known analgesic is aspirin. It is used to reduce fever and inflammation, and to remove aches in your muscles, joints or head.

Aspirin is made from salicylic acid, a chemical that can be acquired from lots of herbs, fruits, grains and even the bark of the willow tree. Clay tablets left by people from 4000 years ago show that willow bark was used for pain relief. It has been a popular part of herbal medicine ever since. But it was only in the 19th century that salicylic acid was manufactured separately as a medicine.

▲ *Modern aspirin was made by the chemical researcher Arthur Eichengrun. The first tablet appeared in 1900 and rapidly became popular in this form*

Arthur Eichengrun

▲ *Arthur Eichengrun (1867–1949)*

Arthur Eichengrun was a Jewish chemist from Germany, known for developing a medicine called Protagol to cure gonorrhoea. The drug fell out of use after more successful antibiotics entered the market. Eichengrun also contributed to the study of plastics and their use, and to the creation of injections.

Eichengrun was a brilliant chemist and material scientist. But his claim to the invention of aspirin was denied due to the prevailing bias against Jewish people. The credit was given to another scientist for several years, until in 1999, when the other disputed claims were closely scrutinised and proven false. Eichengrun was once again credited with the invention of aspirin.

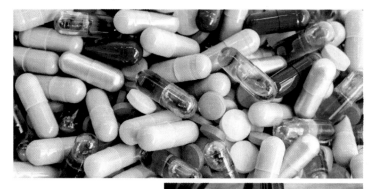

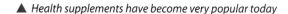

▲ *Health supplements have become very popular today*

In Real Life

Many over-the-counter (OTC) supplements are considered to be marketing gimmicks. There is not enough research to support their health benefits. Do not buy medicines without a doctor's prescription. Always read the labels carefully to confirm that you are buying the correct medication.

Health Supplements

Products such as multivitamin tablets, fish oil, probiotic drinks and certain energy drinks are known as health supplements. Some vitamin and mineral tablets are also used as medicines. For instance, pregnant women in Asian countries are often given iron supplements to combat anaemia. Many people lack Vitamin D and take it in the form of supplements. Doctors also prescribe vitamin supplements to go along with antibiotics. This is because strong antibiotics can harm healthy cells and the vitamins help in restoration.

Sussing out Surgery

Often, acute injuries and illnesses cannot be treated by simply taking medicines. In such cases, doctors may open the affected part of the body and physically set things right.

Specially trained doctors called surgeons operate in specially equipped rooms called Operation Rooms (OR). They work under sanitised conditions to repair any damage and remove infected parts from inside the body.

In Real Life

During a heart attack, a person's heart stops beating. To revive it, doctors send an electric shock through the heart using a device called the defibrillator.

▲ *A skull showing evidence of the practice of trepanation*

◀ *Many modern surgeries are performed by robot arms, which are controlled by a surgeon using a computer. This helps doctors perform very precise and delicate operations.*

6500–3000 BCE
A form of surgery called trepanation (drilling a hole in the skull) is done by ancient humans in France. The purpose of this procedure is not yet known.

335–280 BCE
Alexandrian physician Herophilus **dissects** human cadavers in public. He is known as the 'father of **anatomy**'.

1452–1519
The multitalented Leonardo da Vinci dissects and draws human bodies with stupendous accuracy.

1728–1793
British surgeon John Hunter carries out groundbreaking studies in human biology. He is called the 'father of modern surgery'.

1735
The first known **appendectomy** takes place.

1792
Napoleon Bonaparte's military surgeon Dominique-Jean Larrey creates an ambulance service for soldiers on the battlefield.

▲ *Larrey's Flying Ambulances would take wounded soldiers to field hospitals, located a few kilometres away from the battle. Before this invention, injured men were simply left on the field until the battle ended*

1818
In Britain, James Blundell performs the first successful transfusion of human blood. He transfers blood from a husband to his wife, soon after childbirth.

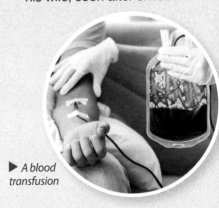

▶ *A blood transfusion*

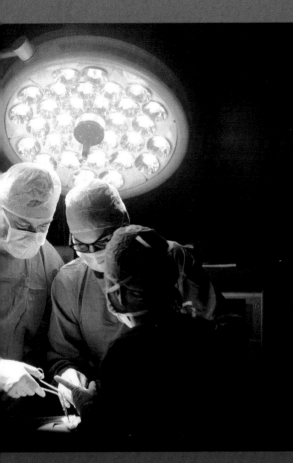

Isn't It Amazing!

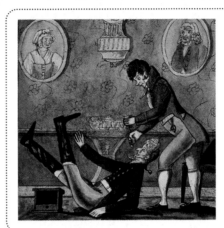

Many ancient cultures, like India, China and Egypt were familiar with surgery. However, in medieval Europe, surgery was done by barbers rather than doctors! In 1540, the United Company of Barber Surgeons of London was set up to finally bring some standards and training to the profession.

◀ *A painting depicting dentistry by a fashionable dentist in 17th century*

1843
Ether is used as an **anaesthetic** for the first time. Four years later, James Simpson uses chloroform as an anaesthetic.

1865
British surgeon Joseph Lister discovers the use of antiseptics in surgery.

1893
The first successful open-heart surgery is performed in the USA, for a wound extremely close to the heart. Three years later, the first successful heart surgery is completed in Germany to repair a stab wound.

1905
The cornea of the eye is transplanted for the first time.

1940
A metal hip replaces bone for the first time.

1937
Blood banks come into being. They aid quicker blood transfusions.

1930
In Germany, a man undergoes an operation to become a woman named Lili Elbe.

1954
A whole organ (a kidney) is transplanted from one body into another. The patient lives on for eight more years.

2008
A laser is used in minimalist keyhole surgery to treat brain cancer.

2013
A successful nerve transfer allows a patient to move their formerly paralysed hand.

Incredible Individuals

Born in 1797, **Dr James Barry** was actually a woman who lived her whole life as a man, because women were not allowed to become surgeons. Dr James Barry became a British military surgeon and, upon her death, was buried as a man.

▶ *Barry's real name was Margaret Ann Bulkley*

Tumours: Benign and Malignant

Our bodies are made of tiny individual units called cells. Healthy cells are able to divide and produce new cells. However, uncontrolled cell growth produces extra lumps of tissue called tumours. Many tumours are benign, that is, they are not presently cancerous and do not spread throughout the body. They can usually be removed by surgery or shrunk using medical procedures. But when tumours continue to grow unchecked and start spreading to other parts of your body, they become dangerous. Such malignant growth is called cancer.

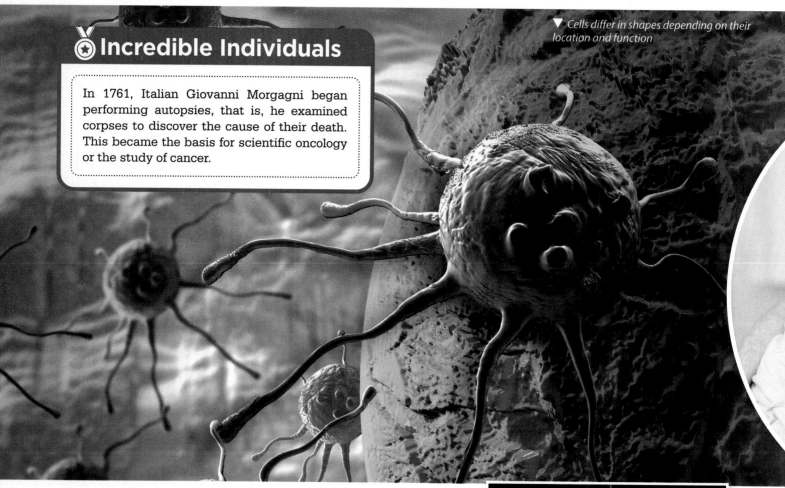

▼ *Cells differ in shapes depending on their location and function*

⭐ Incredible Individuals

In 1761, Italian Giovanni Morgagni began performing autopsies, that is, he examined corpses to discover the cause of their death. This became the basis for scientific oncology or the study of cancer.

🔍 Cancer Treatment

For most of human history, cancer was thought to be untreatable. This changed in the 19th century with the works of physicians Theodor Billroth, Sampson Handley and William Halstead. Working independently, they discovered how cancers spread and how surgery could be used to successfully remove the ailing tissue.

Nowadays, surgical procedures are supported by other methods of cancer removal. In cryosurgery, liquid nitrogen (an extremely cold substance) is sprayed on abnormal cells to freeze and kill them. Sometimes, lasers are used to burn away the cancer. Yet another method places a small antenna inside the tumour. Radio waves are then sent to this receiver, which heats up and kills the cancer cells.

▶ *In Photodynamic Therapy, the patient is given a light-sensitive drug that can kill cancer cells. The doctor then shines a special type of light near the tumour. This activates the drug and destroys the abnormal tissue*

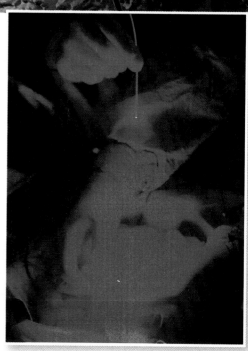

In Real Life

There are many reasons why healthy cells suddenly become cancerous. These include smoking, drinking alcohol, eating junk and foods containing saturated fat, lack of exercise, exposure to radiation, living in polluted air and infection by certain viruses. On the other hand, eating fruits and vegetables can contribute in the fight to prevent cancer. In particular, broccoli and cauliflower have strong anti-cancer compounds.

▲ A balanced diet and regular exercise lead to a healthy lifestyle, which helps prevent cancer

Chemotherapy

During WWII, scientists in the US army discovered a compound called nitrogen mustard, which stopped a type of cancer. Soon after, American doctor Sidney Farber discovered aminopterin, a chemical that is similar to Vitamin B9 (folic acid). He found that this chemical worked against blood cancer in children. This became the first step in identifying more drugs that could be used against cancer. The use of such chemicals is called chemotherapy.

In the 20th century, doctors would first remove cancers through surgery. Then, radiation would be applied to control growths that could not be operated on. Finally, chemotherapy would be used to kill tumours that could not be removed through surgery or radiation.

Immunotherapy

Doctors are studying vaccines that help our natural immune system remove cancer. In 2018, the Nobel Prize for Medicine was awarded to James P. Allison and Tasuku Honjo, for their work in this field. Unlike other vaccines, which are given before an infection, some cancer vaccines are given after the disease is diagnosed.

▲ While destroying cancer, chemotherapy also affects healthy cells. As a result, some patients experience hair loss, vomiting, diarrhoea and anaemia

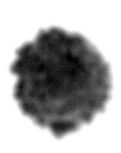
▲ Dr James P. Allison

▲ Dr Tasuku Honjo

Creating Living Tissue

It is fascinating to see living things' abilities and limits of regeneration. For instance, why can you regrow skin if you get a small wound, but not a whole arm if it gets cut off? There are other life forms whose regenerative abilities are much stronger than those of humans.

🔍 In Nature

Some lizards can regrow tails, sharks can make new teeth, and starfish can rebuild their entire body at times. In theory, if we had such regenerative powers, we could live very long, healthy lives. As a result, scientists have been trying to manufacture life in a lab for a very long time.

▶ *In 1996, the sheep Dolly became the first mammal to be created in a lab. She was made using a cell from a ewe. She is, therefore, a clone (a copy) of her 'mother' and has no father*

▲ At the centre of a cell is the nucleus, which is its command centre. When a cell divides into two, the nucleus produces a full copy of itself so that each new cell ends with one complete nucleus

🔍 Creation and Regrowth

With the discovery of cells, scientists began to get a clearer idea of how bodies heal and grow. In 1907, American scientist Ross Granville Harrison grew embryonic frog cells in a lab. This was the first-ever lab cultivation of biological tissue! But it was not until 1981 that tissue culture was used in practical medicine. This happened when biologists from the Eugene Bell Centre for Regenerative Biology and Tissue Engineering repaired wounds using artificial skin made from the patient's own cells. During the 80s, developing biological structures to replace damaged body parts came to be known as tissue engineering.

Incredible Individuals

Thomas Hunt Morgan (1866–1945) studied evolution, genetics and embryology. He worked with fruit flies to show how genetic traits like eye colour are inherited through chromosomes, which is the name for the structures within a cell's nucleus. For his amazing discoveries in genetics, he won a Nobel Prize in **Physiology** or Medicine.

Stem Cells

In 1963, two Canadian scientists named James Till and Ernest McCulloch discovered a new type of cell in the bone marrow of mice. These became known as **stem cells**. Stem cells are unique because they can grow into any other type of cell in the body.

In Till and McCulloch's mice, the stem cells grew into different kinds of blood cells. Researchers are thus interested in these cells because they can be used to replace damaged or dying tissue in the body. They are being studied for diseases that affect the brain, the heart and many other organs. In 2010, a person who had injured their spinal cord became the first to receive embryonic stem-cell treatment.

▲ *The Mexican axolotl is a salamander that can regrow parts of its brain, heart, lower jaw, tail and missing limbs*

3D Bioprinting

In 1983, engineer Chuck Hull built a machine that could print physical objects. Instead of ink, it used plastic-like strands to create objects that you could hold in your hand. By the late 90s, scientists were trying to use it to print human tissue.

In 1999, a bladder was successfully printed on a framework of the patient's own cells. In 2002, a small but functional kidney became the first complex organ to be printed. In 2010, a company called Organovo printed the first blood vessel. Doctors are even aiming to transplant a fully functional printed organ, in the near future.

▶ *In a famous talk in 2011, Dr Anthony Atala held out a kidney that was printed by a 3D printer. The machine used MRI photos of the patient's actual kidney to spray layer after layer of human cells and create a new kidney*

Medical Aid

A great number of medical inventions make daily life better for ailing and ageing people. These range from spectacles and hearing aids to more sophisticated inventions that regulate your heartbeat or clean your body's waste.

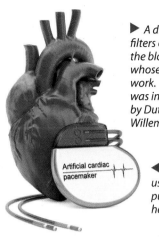

Artificial cardiac pacemaker

◀ The pacemaker uses electrical pulses to regulate heartbeats

▶ A dialysis machine filters out waste from the blood of patients whose kidneys do not work. The first dialyser was invented in 1943 by Dutch doctor Willem Kolff

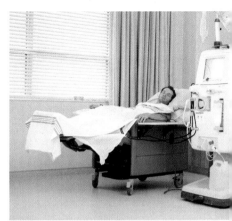

🔍 Wheelchairs

Stone carvings from ancient China and paintings on Greek vases show people on wheeled devices. The earliest known wheelchair made specifically for a disabled person was in 1595. It belonged to King Phillip II of Spain.

In 1655, German watchmaker Steven Farffler made a self-propelled wheelchair for himself. Modern wheelchairs date from the 19th century. The first electric models were created by George Klein to help WWII veterans.

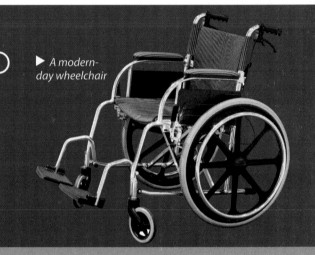

▶ A modern-day wheelchair

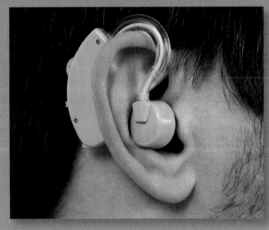

▲ An electrical hearing aid

🔍 Hearing Aids

A hearing aid is a gadget that amplifies the volume of sounds coming to the ear. Early hearing aids looked like trumpets. They had one wide end to collect as much sound as possible. The other, narrow end delivered sound into the ear.

The first electronic hearing aids were also very large. They had to be kept on tabletops and were not easy to move around with. They had large batteries which only lasted for a couple of hours. However, as technology advanced, the aids became small enough to fit inside the ear. Hearing aids today consist of a microphone, an amplifier (which increases the electrical current for a louder sound) and an earphone.

🔍 Lenses

Lenses are curved pieces of transparent materials (like glass) that allow people to see more clearly. The first pair of modern spectacles—with two lenses and short arms going over the ears—was invented in the 18th century by an Englishman. Bifocals were developed around the same time.

The American leader Benjamin Franklin was among the first people to use bifocals. The first non-glass lenses were made of acrylic (a type of plastic) in the late 1940s. However, acrylic was not an ideal substitute for glass. It was only in 1962 that a proper lightweight, long-lasting plastic lens was manufactured.

▶ Before 1000 CE, monks used dome-shaped bits of magnifying glasses called reading stones to read texts

◀ *The first wearable glasses were invented towards the end of the 13th century, most likely by an Italian. They were balanced on top of the nose*

▼ *Bifocals are lenses that are divided into two parts—the bottom part for long-sightedness (or hypermetropia) and the top part for nearsightedness (or myopia)*

👤 In Real Life

Nowadays, contact lenses are a popular alternative to spectacles. They were first conceptualised by Leonardo da Vinci. The first contact lenses were made from glass in 1887. Modern plastic contact lenses were first seen in the 1930s.

🔍 Artificial Limbs

The Roman general Marcus Sergius lost his right hand in the Second Punic War. He later replaced it with an iron hand, built to hold a shield so that he could continue fighting. This is one of the first known cases of a prosthetic (artificial) limb.

In the 16th century, French doctor Ambroise Paré invented hinged hands and locking knees. Modern prosthetics are also made of lighter, stronger materials like carbon polymers and plastics. Often, they are fitted with electronics that allow for better control over actions such as gripping, walking, jumping, etc.

▶ *A prosthetic leg crafted for an athlete*

▲ *An electronically controlled prosthetic leg*

What is a Transplant?

In medicine, a transplant (or a graft) means taking tissue from its original location and using it to heal some other part of the body. It can be done with an entire organ or with some part of it. When a tissue is grafted from one part of your body to another part of your own body, it is called an autograft. Organ transplants are also made from one human being to another.

The History of Autograft

As far back as the sixth century BCE, surgeons in the Indian subcontinent were practising tissue grafts. Specifically, they could rebuild shattered noses using skin flaps from the patient's arm. The flap would remain attached to the arm until the nose area grew new blood vessels. After about two to three weeks, the arm would be freed from the nose.

This method spread to Western medicine in the 16th century through the efforts of Italian surgeon Gaspare Tagliacozzi.

▼ *The Sushruta Samhita, an ancient Indian text, outlines the process of skin grafts*

⊛ Incredible Individuals

Alexis Carrell developed groundbreaking ways to sew blood vessels together, for which he received the Nobel Prize in Medicine in 1912. His work laid the foundation for organ transplant surgery. In 1990, Joseph Murray received the Nobel Prize for his revolutionary work in advancing organ transplants using radiotherapy and immunosuppressants. He shared it with Donnall Thomas, who invented methods of providing bone marrow cells for transplant.

▶ *Alexis Carrell*

Transplant Successes

The body's immune system treats most transplants as foreign bodies and attacks them. All transplants—even autografts and transplants between identical twins—are prone to such rejection. To prevent this situation from arising, transplant recipients are given drugs called immunosuppressants, which help the body successfully cope with the transplant.

In the Western world, the first successful transplant was a skin graft performed in Denmark in 1870. It was not until 1954 that a whole organ, a kidney, was transplanted. Dr Joseph Murray, who performed the surgery on two identical twins, received a Nobel Prize in 1990.

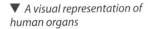

▼ *A visual representation of human organs*

Facts about Transplants

▲ *In 1969, Thomas Starzl performed a successful liver transplant. In the same year, Christiaan Barnard completed the first successful heart transplant*

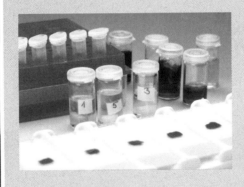

Before any transplant, samples of blood and tissue are taken from the donor and recipient. These are checked to see how well they match. Since 1977, computers have assisted in the organ-matching process. Many countries now keep state-wide or nation-wide systems of donor information.

In 1981, a combination heart-lung transplant was successfully executed by renowned surgeon Bruce Reitz.	In 1998, a full hand was successfully transplanted for the first time. The surgery was done in France.	A partial face transplant was also first successfully performed in France. Five years later, in 2010, a full-face transplant was achieved in Spain.

Genetics

Have you ever wondered why the biologically related members of a family look like each other? The answer lies in the nucleus of the cell. This dark nucleus is made up of microscopic matter called genes. The study of genes is called genetics. Genes give our cells their basic form and function.

Children inherit genes from their parents. Thus, they look like a mix of their parents, and can also resemble their siblings, grandparents, aunts, uncles, cousins, etc. Genes decide the colour of a flower, give the lion its mane and differentiate a fish from a bird.

DNA

Genes are made up of a chemical called deoxyribonucleic acid or DNA. Lots of DNA and protein come together to form thread-like structures called chromosomes. Different creatures have a different number of chromosomes. A garden pea has 14 chromosomes and an elephant has 56. DNA itself has a peculiar shape called a double-helix. This was discovered by scientists Francis Crick and James Watson in the 1950s.

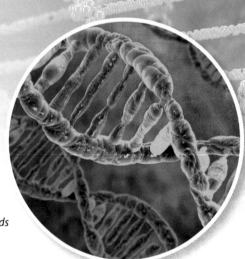

▶ *The double-helix DNA is formed by two entwined strands*

Human Genome Project (HGP)

A genome is the genetic make-up of an organism. Over 1990–2003, the Human Genome Project (HGP) identified and published all the thousands of genes that make up a human being. Going forward, this will help doctors and scientists understand how to improve human life, especially how to reverse ageing and cure inherited diseases.

⊙ Incredible Individuals

In 1962, Crick, Watson and Maurice Wilkins won a Nobel Prize for discovering the structure of the DNA. However, they could not have done it without Rosalind Franklin's work. It was Franklin who obtained the images of DNA. She did so using X-ray techniques, which tragically led to her death by cancer. When the prize was awarded, Franklin—most unfairly—was left out!

▲ *Dr Francis Crick*   ▲ *Dr James Watson*

▲ *Dr Maurice Wilkins*

▲ *Dr Rosalind Franklin*

Royal Rarities

Royalty has always considered itself special. In an effort to keep their blood 'pure', members of royal families often married their relatives. Eventually, they became so interrelated, new marriages were taking place between cousins. This is called inbreeding. It sometimes results in people being born with rare and tragic defects.

Haemophilia

The most infamous 'royal disease' was haemophilia. It occurs when blood clots do not form to stop a wound from bleeding. The illness affected many male descendants of Queen Victoria of England. She married her first cousin, Prince Albert. Their son Leopold fell and hurt himself. He died from blood loss. Through her daughters, haemophilia spread to other royal families of Europe. The two sons of the German Kaiser Wilhelm II, as well as the son of the Russian Tsar Nicholas II, were all haemophiliacs.

▲ After 16 generations of inbreeding, the royal Habsburg family of Europe started showing physical deformities. The Habsburg Jaw, seen here in Charles II of Spain, is the name for a jutting lower jaw—usually under a thick lower lip

Porphyria

Another disease of the blood, porphyria comes in different forms. James V of Scotland most likely passed it to his daughter Mary, Queen of Scots. She suffered from ulcers, mental illnesses, physical disablement and rheumatism since her teens. Her son James I of England had urine as 'purple as Alicante wine'—another sign of porphyria. Their descendent George III, nicknamed 'Mad' King George, would wander through the castle, blind, deaf and dirty. Unable to recognise anyone, he was sadly neglected by his caretakers. In 1810, his son forced his removal from the throne.

In Real Life

King Henry VIII of England suffered from the very common disease, malaria. The first cure for malaria was found in South America. A feverish man, desperate with thirst, drank from a pool of water and was cured. He noticed that the water was bitter. It had been 'poisoned' by the surrounding cinchona trees. Over the 18th and 19th centuries, scientists found and purified the chemical from the tree. It is called quinine and is used to cure malaria to this day.

▲ A painting of George III of Great Britain commissioned during his younger, happier days

Word Check

Anaesthetic: It is a drug that numbs a part of your body (local anaesthetic) or puts your whole body to sleep (general anaesthetic).

Analgesic: It is a painkiller.

Anatomy: It is the study of the internal structure of living things.

Antibiotics: They are used to kill dangerous bacteria.

Appendectomy: It is the surgical removal of the appendix, a small pouch-like organ in the lower right side of your abdomen.

Bilirubin: It is a yellowish substance formed in the liver. It gives its colour to human excrement.

Biopsy: It is a test where tissue is removed from a living person to check for the cause or presence of disease.

Dermatoscope: It is a device used to examine the lesions on a patient's skin.

Dissect: It is a process by which a person methodically cuts open a dead creature (plant, animal or human) to study its insides.

ECG: It is the abbreviation for electrocardiogram. It is a test that records your heartbeat to see if it is functioning well.

EEG: It is the abbreviation for electroencephalogram. It is a test for examining abnormalities in your brain.

Electromagnetic rays: A number of visible and invisible rays that include X-rays, all the colours of light, microwaves, infrared rays, gamma rays and many others

Epidemic: It refers to the spreading of an infectious disease to a large number of people.

Germ theory: It is a medical theory stating that some diseases are caused by the presence of microorganisms (organisms that can only be seen through a microscope).

Obstetrics: It is the field of medicine that is concerned with childbirth.

Ophthalmoscope: It is the medical device used to look into a patient's eye.

Otoscope: It is the medical device that doctors use to look into a patient's ears.

Photomicrography: It refers to photographing a substance while it is kept under a microscope.

Physiology: It is the way a living being and its body parts function.

Porphyria: It is a disease affecting the blood and nervous system.

Retina: The part of your eye that receives information from light rays and transmits it to the brain

Sphygmomanometer: A device that measures blood pressure

Stem cell: An undifferentiated cell that can turn into a specialised cell at a later point

Variolation: It is an obsolete technique of immunising a patient.